THE SWANS OF PERGUSA

Other books by Peter Shaindlin

Citizen Steele, first edition (2012)

Citizen Steele, second edition (2015)

Joys & Sorrows

18 Passions

❈ ❈ ❈

THE
SWANS
of
PERGUSA

PETER SHAINDLIN

DEUXMERS

Published by Deuxmers, LLC
PO Box 440, Waimanalo, Hawaii

Book & cover design by Ara Feducia

Printed in the United States of America
ISBN 978-0-9835041-6-0
First edition, June 2015

For N.

Omnia mutantur, nihil interit

– Publius Ovidius Naso

CONTENTS

PREFACE

Publius Ovidius Naso (Ovid) was the great Roman romantic. He loved his Rome but in the end, no god or goddess appeared to save or vindicate him as in the mythological tales he so graciously memorialized. His personal tragedy—banishment from Rome, the city he adored—bore hallmarks of the very stories he told, Shakespearean in their humanitarian manifestations a millennium-and-a-half before his spiritual successor imbued upon Western society his own omniscient perceptions of the human stain. As with his subsequent Elizabethan counterpart, Ovid's contributions bore over time at least as much impact on future generations as they did upon his own. His discreetly whimsical poesy transformed the expressive literary conventions of the time: while he preceded them each by centuries, he magnificently captured the future rustic lyrical touch of Cervantes and in subtle moments the caustic wit and humor of Samuel Johnson. This collection is really but a retelling of stories recounted so many times before in the oral tradition of the Roman poet Ovid's time. The mellifluous pulse and rhythm of the tales in his vast epic *Metamorphoses* is at once compelling and intoxicating.

A concurrent source of inspiration for this book was *Tales from Ovid* by the late British Poet Laureate Ted Hughes, an exquisite, symphonic homage that celebrates Ovid at least as much as *Metamorphoses* itself. Hughes' wry translation from the Latin of some twenty-four selected passages was the evolutionary bridge from which *The Swans of Pergusa* was born. In one way, Hughes' balletic work constitutes an emotional and sociological investigation informing the purpose and nature of Ovid's original creation. *Metamorphoses* itself is introduced with striking biblical parallels: a lengthy prelude sequentially catalogues the creation of the universe: earth, man and his deities distinct from eventual Hebrew and Christian dogma with the notion of plurality in the Godhead. The principal hallmarks of collective Western mythologies—power and rule, gods, loyalty, love, deceit, comedy and tragedy—are arranged by Ovid in dazzling virtuosic display, the entirety of the human condition laid out in compelling harmony with nature itself—earthly elements playing central roles in the dramas for which they are also the stage. Ovid presents mankind in a persuasive Aristotelian argument of remarkable grandeur. Pyramus and Thisbe are metaphorically, painfully separated by walls and fissures, ceremoniously gravitating towards vibrant natural idols of trees and dales; Actaeon is adrift in the very forest that spawns the creatures which will turn to devour him; Pygmalion's creator literally attempts bringing art to life. This deep reverence for the astonishments of the natural world is the intrinsic behavioral lodestar in the Roman gene that counterbalances an otherwise blunt, linear societal tendency towards violence and conquest: domination as the central collective tendency of a culture.

In sharp contrast with Hellenist qualities, Ovid's Rome did not in any sense reflect an abstract philosophical bent; on the contrary, its communal zeitgeist was all about what one did versus who one was. *Veni, vidi, vici* was in stark contrast to the subsequent ruminations of Descartes who focused on the self versus collective culture, a preamble to romanticism from social and artistic perspectives. And but yet, Ovid was a romantic in the time of Caesar, born within one year of history's most infamous assassination. He was out of place and out of time, yet of his time.

The behavior of the Roman gods afforded ostensible explanations for what existed; Ovid however was concerned *a priori* with consequences. For him, both justice and injustices were givens in society; the real conundrum was, how does one *manage* what fate has thrust upon him? There certainly was no generalized if plausible answer.

For Midas, all the world turned to gold — which destroyed him, while, despite her sanctified spirit, Proserpina is victimized by rape. How does one cope with such incidents; how should one respond? In the case of Ovid himself, notwithstanding the many implied lessons within the stories of the gods he so beautifully explored, there was no solution per se; his own exile to what is now Romania is considered by some a legendary metaphor for injustice. In addition to the anguish of cultural isolation, he lamented in letters to friends that living in that non-Latin speaking society, he found himself cut off as well from the language from which the figurative melodies of his literary compositions intrinsically derived. Alas, our exiled Roman found himself in the position of what centuries later would represent the classic plight of the rejected romantic. For all of its conspicuous faults, he was certainly more content within the trappings of Rome given his love of its culture, than was say Shelley in England, effectively banishing himself. At any rate, it is not uncommon for an artist to experience some sort of lèse-majesté during his creative evolutions as precursor to both his artistic growth and societal decline, and often simultaneously. Shelley however thrived in his risqué, uncharted new environment while Ovid withered — yet he still had his gods.

With many great works of literary art, their ultimate beauty truly lies in the grandeur, fluidity and palpable "rhythm" of the overall opus, separate of content yet at the same time, inextricably bound to it. For centuries poets were in a sense self-restricted by virtue of established standards in metered structure; in the case of the Romans and so for Ovid, it was the prevailing dactylic hexameter of "epic poetry" that set the general conventions for his work. In terms of literal rhythm it was quite specific, dictating quantitative meter and syllabic length throughout. Freedom can only emerge from structure and as such, a common standard was set that provided a point of differentiation, thus allowing individual styles to emerge between artists.

This sort of "pre-structured" framework greatly affects the selection of words by the poet, or at the very least, of synonyms. Initially as with a dance, the steps "control" the dancer, until eventually as he masters the style he has the opportunity to transcend the medium itself.

Rhythm can also reveal itself *between* sections of works just as it does more microcosmically between syllables, words or stanzas. Proust's *À la recherche du temps perdu* is at once a masterpiece of fiction while also a staggering chronicle of transforming social eras. Yet on a purely artistic plane and notwithstanding its seven volumes, it can also be perceived as a kind of "grand sonata" with respect to the structure of classically rooted symphonic form. In considering for example the later portions of the work, one volume ends with a tragic "pastoral" in which the hero Swann finds himself virtually ignored during his announcement of cancer to questionably "close" friends, concluding the adagio episode under a shroud of woeful lamentation. Contrastingly, the first page of the subsequent volume has all the frantic excitement of a scherzo as the perverse Charlus appears like a strutting peacock in a Parisian courtyard to engage in a wanton exchange of body language with Jupien the tailor before together they speedily disappear. As the work nears its conclusion the story lunges some years forward to the bombing of Paris during the Great War, literally exploding with bombastic fury and intensity towards its final, remarkable allegro apotheosis. *Metamorphoses* bears similar overarching rhapsodic qualities in terms of grand rhythmic schemes; as was the case with Proust, Ovid surely knew that he was forging his own magnum opus, precisely because it celebrated and memorialized his *world*—one which in the end he would never return to. Subscribing to Margaret Atwood's view that rhythm precedes meaning, I have chosen not to set the natural flow of words within any sort of fixed meter.

I composed these poems simply because I was interested, and also as it gives me pleasure to share their beauty with the uninitiated. For those more knowledgeable than me in the genre, or Ovid specifically, and as presumptuously as was likely the case with Hughes, I hope that this new telling might bring refreshing light to these astonishing, timeless tales.

Rather than separating his mythical poems, Ovid allowed them to blend together as naturally as the tales themselves, also justified by the sequential interpolation of related characters and events between each. *The Swans of Pergusa* is a random grouping of ten of the many more myths he shared and fewer than the collection assembled by Hughes, which itself was a significant reduction in breadth from that of *Metamorphoses*.

In *Epilogues*, each earlier tale is briefly revisited with a view towards unleashing its more primeval essence; mythical emotion—its essential tonality as I subjectively discerned it in my readings of Ovid's original poems that the virtuosic Hughes reinterpreted two thousand years later — during which he searched for the atom. In *Epilogues* I sought to split it.

Peter Shaindlin
Honolulu, January 2015

THE
SWANS
of
PERGUSA

CREATION - THE FOUR AGES - GIANTS - LYCAON - THE FLOODS

Chaos was the world

All within it was tumult—
There was no sphere, no core, no light—
Even darkness had not yet
Collected its shadows
Nor was there an up and down
Nor in or out,
Nor essence

It was a lovely absence of things
We came to know after the floods

What sat freely
Within the vastness of nothingness
Was one great endless, silent mass
That always was,

And gathered all eternities
Within its fold:
The bank of souls
Which had not yet released
First breath upon the universe

Earth, sea and sky were one

Within these were all the colors,
Yet they were trapped
Within the endless, weightless thing
That had not yet been touched by Jupiter

God and nature then were one—
He was the only consciousness,
With no living things to rule

There was no heat, nor cold nor sun
There was no sound or taste, or even darkness

In this place so lacking things
There also was no pain or lust—
There was no flame or pressing sea;

No wind, no heights, no sultry depths

No woman
No man
No jealousy—

Until the first and most supreme
Appeared

His vision was of earth, sea and sky

He swung his right arm 'round
—It was a massive limb
That, as it moved,
Stirred such gusts throughout heaven
That entire planets
Were tossed off their course
And the galaxy itself
Rocked like a buoyed gyroscope

The great God called upon powers from without himself:
Great, faceless demiurge,
Release yourself;

Give us your gifts
Of water and of matter

He created his new children:
Rivers, streams, broad estuaries
Mountains and cliffs above the newborn sea
That framed the edge of lands
Where no animal and no man
Had yet tread

With joyous heart
He reached within his flowing robe
And tossed hands high;
A million flecks of brilliant gold,
Rising upward, glittering

—He called them stars

They could only be discerned
By He, the sole creator—
For there was not yet a sun
By which its brilliant rays
Could pierce the darkness below them
And be seen by those of breath
That would follow

He reached right down
And with great force
Spun this mass of chaos
So willfully
That it did turn
As if on a potter's wheel
And round by round
Took on the form of potent orb

Its motion was divine—
Land, ocean and heavens
First knew their place
And lived together

Sheer magnetic energies
Conjured by his magnum works
Were of so great a tempest's roar
That all the elements now birthed

Resonated with such frenzy
That a star above which he had thrown
Saw earth below
And could not help but weep
At its sweet loveliness

This slab, so moved by nature's glint
Could not simply sit and turn—
In one frightening, violent burst
It blew apart and,
Burning yellow fire,
Threw light on the many spheres
That danced about it in shadows
And hence were called the planets

Now, with this sun—
A dying star,
The many lands that lay fallow
Begin to feel the heat of dawn,
Bathed in porous, wondrous light
From heaven's vaults
Like spilt treasure,
Cosseting seeds from earth's first trees
Which, drinking of the virgin dew
Sprouted forth a thousand flowers—

Ranunculus and lavender,
Heather, hydrangea
Daphne teeming

—All of which had wrapped themselves
About the meadows skirting seas—
Blazing hues, a palate bright
Upon which bees appeared
And laced their smoothest nectar
O'er the lips of Jupiter

Next he thought to introduce
A rhythm by which time could flow:
Waving his great spear through clouds
He stroked it to and fro
Until four parts were seen;
The first and third would undulate
Between a warmth and chill each year
The second burned with scorching air
While very last the rain did freeze
And shower its clear ornaments
Delicately on the land
Until it came to rest and form
A milky, frozen silver bed
Washing all these things in white

The first part would return
To start the cycle yet once more,
And with no end

Until the world would die

With all this done
Jupiter, well satisfied
Looked down upon the place he'd shaped
And now, Prometheus unleashed
Took his turn to craft a thing
That was the first to take
From all else cast:

He gave it man
Who, very first,
Before he moved, or walked, or spoke
Begin his life the way he does:
By drawing in a hearty breath—

Then he took man
And of him gave us woman
By painting man with roses
And splashing him
With potent scents

A third kind
He also brought to bear
Which, different from man
And nothing of woman
Was beheld by those first genders
As so abhorrent and debased
That, fearing discord and chagrin
The great God, with one sweep of titanic foot
Dashed away that thing that never more would be

And nature roared
That that from which it was taken—
Its lovely, sacred oxygen
Had been withdrawn
From all the rest
That sat so long in perfect bliss:

Sin was born,
Destroying earth
More gradually than it was wont

So that man could have a place
As he could not make his own,
Great Jupiter
Picked up grand globs of soil
And massive stones,
Tossing them from up on high
Down upon the cold bleak earth
To form with grace yet randomly
The continents that gave to man
A place of height above the seas

He blew a long and steady breath
Around the globe
That curled and spun in different forms
About the hills and gentle dales
To form in some a misty shroud
Of pungent fog

While southern lands and islets small
It buffered to permit the sun
To wash them in its dazzling ways

Gazing down to see his work,
He shed upon them endless tears
Of joy and hope

Cascading down in sheets like glass
They washed the colder lands that formed
—He called it rain

Man was quick to master tongues
And with that came such babel
That Prometheus asked Jupiter
To squelch their sounds and cries and songs
For he could no longer sleep or rest
In such cacophony

So his God, in further inspired state
Bestowed upon the lands
Five thousand different animals
With two of each
So that they could replace themselves

Thus began the Golden Age—
There was no conflict:
Love was the only thing

And man knew
The song of nature,
Pristine rhapsodies

No wars were known
No masters, slaves—
Therefore no punishment;
Violence had not reared its head

Even basest animals
Did not fight
—They knew the mysteries of silence

Man's love was the harvest;
Rivers flowed of honey
Where maidens dipped their buckets
To capture bees' sweet nectar

Finches gazed down to see
Children pushing moistened bulbs
Within the loam
Bands of heather and lilac
Washed the hillsides in spring

In summer, poppy flowers burst forth
And in a ravine
Where falling water formed sweet pools
A red-haired maiden,
Destined a goddess

Bathed her breasts
With milk of the dogwood flower

All was peace—
Until the Age of Silver came
And with it
Came the force of seasons

Frigid zephyrs off the northern mounts
Rolled vast sheets of iced air
Down onto the plains,
Across the valleys,
Laying their chill upon the backs of men
Like sharpened swords in winter

Fire, tamed to heat the cave
And rouse the grain
Threw light upon the night
Where before man had rested and slept
Without the need to see
What he knew lay before him

Then came the Age of Brass—
It hardened the hearts of men
To match the density and spiteful mass
Of hills and crags they called their towns

But still, as in three ages yore
A common bond

Did hold together all of souls,
Across oceans
And nations
And generations

The Age of Iron smote the earth
And plunged it into frothing evil

Fire, steel, even stones—
All were repurposed

Objects of nature, elements
Transformed to weaponry—
Man turned on man
Nation turned on nation
Even man turned on woman—
Because he could

Fate sealed at the hands of the strong
Who took the things they never should

For the first time
Spring and summer knew dark days;
Rain would fall on top of rain
Until the plains would flood,
Their harvest lost

Cunningness was born:
New weaponry emerged—

Deception, harm, treachery
All became the ways of gain
Personified by the transformation of their god
Into a king with plagues of man:
Thunderous hell, tainted hearts

Possession was the arbiter
Of life and want;
Everything was owned—
The land, the ships, the towns, the goods, the stalls—
Buttons on a child's coat

Each day man rose
And dreamed of reaching dusk
With more in his arms than at the dawn

No one was free of menace:
Even great Jupiter in his lofty haunts
Was one day assailed by stomping giants
Who marched in form straight up the highest mountaintops
Which, like huge stairs
Led to the golden gates of his great throne

Seizing molten thunderbolts
He one-by-one pierced their icy hearts
The force and might that took to wind
By way of all his stirrings
Exploded Mount Olympus
Which, upon the closing of its plumes

Did scatter so much ash
That every giant thing
Was buried deep, forever more

Worse though came next
A race of creatures formed of sludge
And murk and stones
Lacking in the things of man
That set him out apart as one:

No hearts, no ears, no tongues, no blood
They rose from the earth
And viewed it all
With three green eyes

Murder alone was their vice—
But whom to kill besides themselves;
They marched up and down through steep gorges
Until they spotted man and knew
That this was their time

Jupiter, god of gods, agonized
At seeing all his handiwork
Within the universe, his home
So bluntly trivialized,
Did summon up his family
That, here till now
Had rested 'bout the heavens
Knowing not of these dark things

Across the sky each danced and weaved,
One leaping through Saturn's rings
As others soared between sleeping moons
Or rode on comets towards earth

On a dais spanning heaven
They sat, leering at the planets
With great apprehension

Their Lord told of his plight—
His godly halls assaulted by monsters,
Easily contained—yet far worse,
A league of misanthropes,
Destruction their only way

The consortium rocked with rage,
Demanding a solution—
But firm Jupiter continued:

Having felt the force of evil
Aimed upon his sacred ground
He'd gone to earth and,
Starting from Olympus' heights
He strode across the land, as man

Looking, watching, seeing, hearing
All the wretched, base results
Of ages fallen down upon

The brink of each before itself,
Until when man had killed his own

With his heart so low and crushed
At seeing his creation stained,
He wandered on,
Traversing the rough steppes of Maenalus
And on to the wells of Arcadia
Above which, on a jagged ridge,
Within an edifice divine
Lived Lycaon, a spiteful king
Who, warmed within its coal-stoked walls
Admitted him before his court

And when this god-as-man did show
A symbol of his deity,
Despite the reverence shown to him
By that sagacious gathering,
Lycaon turned and scowled aside,
Declaring he soon would test
How valid was the nomad's claim

Night soon fell and after grub
They each retired to their rooms
Jupiter, disguise retained
Rested while he thought about
The course to take upon this king

Meanwhile, in the steaming bowels
Below the structure's sleeping suites
The crazed king seized a slave
Whom he had bled and sliced alive
Upon which time
He laced his parts
Into the paste of a grand stew
Prepared by his legion
And offered it up to the god disguised
Who, with his special powers
Saw through this awful sham
Perpetrated upon him
And in his rage
Stomped his feet with such anger
That the earth wobbled on its axis
While great deep gunmetal clouds formed high

Within these storms
Great stabs of light—
Electric bolts,
Rambling miles of pulsing shafts
Struck straight through the chest of the Arcadian despot—
Such was the charge that ran through his torso
That his mind exploded into weeds,
Sprung up as if a scrappy field

He wandered the earth evermore
Mind ablaze with lunacy—
Maniacal lupus
Forever chasing flocks of fleece

It was now the mind of Jupiter
That every human house,
Toxic and vile,
Should suffer
With its own destructive air

He thus proposed this to his court
Who, torn between a wealth of facts
And fear of man fully gone,
Leaving nothing but a mass not so unlike
That which had formed before him,
Objected to his scheme
To crush his human spawn

And so he did retreat
Within his halls
For many days
To contemplate
A way in which all of man
Would learn and earn humility—

It was at the hands of nature
That he found a voice that,
With its form and force
Would steal and shape
The course of men:

On the very first day of the hundredth year
He, from his supreme high perch
Waved his arm with such great might
That all the planets bobbed and weaved
Like jetsam
Spewed across a frothing sea
In stormy maelstrom,
Away from their normal course

With ferocious magnetism
All their metals alchemized;
Transmuted from mere spinning spheres,
Their gravitation altered thus—

Great storms did fall upon the earth—
Mountains split by liquid force,
Their inner magma brought to bear
Upon each town and hamlet
Caught within their racy course

Ignis stone;
Leaping heat across the valleys' loins
Had men fast-footed,
Fleeing for their cursed lives

The seas were swept up in great foaming sheets—
Briny, tepid air,
Until they flipped upon their backs
Tossing upwards sharks and snails,

Squatina, Zebrus zebrus, Mora moro;
Bramble sharks and Salmo salar
Flipped their fins in open air,
Gasping gills devoid of mist

Vulcan rose from under Etna
Soaring like a giant tree—
With a shake of his great shoulders
Lands fractured
Across the continents,
Shattered plates beneath the seas
Forming abysses
Into which higher oceans
Spilled themselves,
Coaxed down by central forces
In the earthly sphere

Acis aided Jupiter
Spilling out her river banks
To such great heights that,
From the cliffs of Sicily
They roared across the top of seas
To strike up upon Adriatic banks
That quickly crumbled
As the raging waves consumed
Each village that they rolled upon
Until the land straight east across
Dalmatian foot lands
Drowned beneath this salty brine

Skies across the falling earth
Were of the closest gray to black
Thousands sank beneath the depths
As all the world was cleansed of sin—
There was no longer avarice
For there was nothing to possess
And few to take possession

The great ice bars
That formed the caps of north and south
Were shattered by vibrations
Of this shuddering orb—
In great chunks they plied the sea,
Motion melting them
To further flood the hinterlands

Dii Consentes, unified
Set their course of craft and trade
Upon the sphere
To aid their Lord
In vanquishing the vile seeds
Of fallen man

Only Mercury,
Supplied by art
Did hesitate
In that he could not acclimate
His heart against a churning world
Of lifelessness

Of Janus, Jupiter expected much
As he was of the portal
That allowed all men to forge anew
And so he stood fast and ready
While Master did his giant works
Until a day might come
When he could cast the sun
To splash its golden rays again
Across the cheeks of citizens
That learned again humility

Men of fleetest foot
Got themselves
Atop the highest, shrinking hills

Under siege of heartless floods,
Their mettle tested to its peak,
They scavenged up crude bivouacs
Against the skies
That breathed chill ire upon them
From dense, rambling clouds

Cities under liquid glass
Visited by gods and goddesses
That swam amongst vast schools of fish,
All peering to and fro
At columns, temples, avenues
Submerged in blue beryl galleries

Of porous ether, submarined—
Drunken, living frescoes
Washed in opaque monotones

Mankind consumed by nature—
Baptized cities

PELEUS AND THETIS

Fearing legacy usurped
Through ascendency
Great Jupiter pressed his lust
Through family

Rape of ocean
By grandchild—
A legacy by keen design

Thetis—queen of marine cathedrals,
Briny shoals lacquered;
Haemonia's supple shores
With dusty lips of blinding sand

Dolphin-borne goddess
Ascended from the foamy depths
To penetrate her cavern home
Tucked in neat upon the sea

Soaked in slumber, naked
To the earth she lay

Flesh on flesh:
Her lips were met
By Peleus

Proteus had painted her
A savage foe

Advised of this phenomenon
He clasped her tight
And, standing firm
Rejected doubt
With purpose clear

Hungry palms and probing mouth
Sampled her and fondled
Fruits of chastity
That withered at his wonton touch

Transformed in rage—
A cat, a hawk, stinging serpent
Panther black

With rigid fangs
Tore at him,
Thrashing, howling too

Hog-tied like a lamb undone
His pungent girth shattered her
And split the sea

His violent seed
Now washed her loins
With milky bliss

Stillborn day—

With sparkling eyes
Thetis gazed at cavern top
And fell in love
With motherhood who,
Wed with lust,
Will always do rapacious deeds,
Divined—
Achilles at its thunderhead

PROSERPINA

Typhon, flat upon his back
Beneath the soil, gargantuan
Legs traversing ocean depths
From Corsica to Sicily

Massive head
Wearing Etna like a crown
Awakened with blazing rage
His tremors shaking mountain through
Where there on high
Sat Aphrodite,
Reminded thus by vantage point—
That only tender, mellow loam
Did separate such earthly things
From Pluto's broad-based underworld

With Cupid's powers she bid him cast
An arrow down beneath the lands
That soared for miles,
Through brackish caves

Until it plunged more fathoms low
And, speeding still,
Ripped through the heart of hell's great king

Pluto wretched and heaved with pain
That just as quickly changed its tone

To blissful pangs of avarice
And hunger for low-hanging fruit

There is a lake like Koenigssee
With placid skin
Yet chilly depths
Pergusa was its name to those
Who played upon its calming shores
Its surface was begat with swans
That skirted nobly to and fro

A girl there, Proserpina,
Daughter of Jove and Ceres,
Cossetted by friends galore

Springtime zephyrs
Rich with pleasant oxygen
Tossed about the butterflies
Whose colors mixed with flower points
Snapped away
And hoisted high by virgin hands

At times a scene of love serene
Is ripped asunder with the speed

Of lightning bolts—yet silence rules
And not until the crime is done
Do others near perceive the deed,
Standing with no remedy

And so it was when Pluto struck,
Seizing maiden rapidly
And swiftly descended
Into the caves of hell

With fiery lance
He split the surface of the lake
And, with his spoils, sunken now—
Of those left screaming at the shore,
Flowers forgotten,
Scattered 'bout their rosy toes

By chariot of burning red
He stole her off unto his home—
A mansion in that dreaded sphere
Within the earth's extensive bowels

No other thoughts could fill this mind
Already brimming over
With rhapsodies of lust and blood

Proserpina shrieked horrid screams
—So shrill, so grieved
A thousand blackbirds fell from the sky

Her mother hearing now the news
Felt grief beyond her wildest dreams
Agony so rude and rank
It deconstructed all her heart
Until, without the breath of life
Her flesh was melted into mists
That, once condensed in colder air
Transmogrified,
Lost amongst the vastness of the ocean's depths

As winter neared
Ceres' porous self one day
Rising to the ocean's top
Vaporized into a cloud
Which, rising high above the mountain's dales
Found itself met by a draft
So chill that rain became her steed
Let free from high to fall that hour
Upon the head of Jupiter, preoccupied
With other things that tempt the gods

But Ceres, showing him her face
Insisted that his fatherhood
Should dictate that he intervene—

A force near hell compelled her to
Continue showering down on earth
Where, certain drops that held her thoughts

Happened to fall back upon
The lake where Arethusa, lovely nymph,
Implored her to forgive the earth
And cease her plague on Sicily—
Where Ceres had placed all her blame

With this she cast up o'er the sun
On chariot
To take on Jove—
Again she pushed him to step in
And save her sweet Proserpina
From the ghastly lair

Conditional he was, to wit:
She could return and start again,
But only if she had not yet
Tasted of the fruit of hell

—Alas, she had:
A pomegranate she had seized—
Her blood was purple now, diseased
Forever then she was allowed
To live in both the skies and depths
For six months here, then six months there
Her heart in bliss
And then despair

PYRAMUS AND THISBE

The four parents of young Pyramus and Thisbe
Forbade their kinship,
Thinking queer their episodes:
Such young children could not know
What makes love real—
But love is pain set to purpose

In two stone houses side-by-side
In Babylon, where earth did shift
A split occurred between the two,
Where light was freed to penetrate
The bifurcated homes within
And touch upon the lovely face
Of Thisbe
Whose sweet honeyed breath
Migrated between the wall
To tweak the nose of Pyramus
Who dizzied at its luscious scent,
Transfixed as well
By Thisbe's great soft hazel eyes
That shimmered
Like almonds of tanzanite

For years this was their conduit
Of love and bond
Beauty was a fractured face,

A muted smile—
Exaltation in many forms

They knew of a mulberry tree
Refracting blazing light off of soft, sweet petals—
The only living thing
In a field of dust approaching jagged hills

Thisbe said,
Meet me there blue Monday,
When gibbous moon
Will bathe that tree in lavender

Under arcing bows
Our hands shall win their race with breath
—Our only wall is time

That fateful night,
In her swiftness, buoyed by love
Young Thisbe reached the valley first

The beating of her supple heart
Was heard by a creature near
Whose soft steps seemed like music—
The sound of Pyramus—
The same soft music
As when he grasped the wall each night

She could not have known
That happiness would end for her this cursed night:
Death sleeps in shadows

From the darkness came a roar
A lioness with furrowed mane
Took vicious swipes
That clawed her skin
And splayed her silken scarf
With crimson blood
That soaked its tattered shreds
Across the ground

Thisbe, wounded, fled to hide
Between two soaring granite cliffs
Tucked within a narrow space
That mirrored splintered fissure
From which at home
She'd whispered lover's words

Pyramus, not knowing this
Came upon the scene
Which, moments before
Savage beast had fled

Heart shattered, spotting bloodied rag,
Envisioning her violent end
Under tree whose graceful limbs
Had formed their canopy of love

He lost all hope and,
Desperate to be with her
Prepared for his dark journey;
Raised his kingdom key up high—
His sterling sword
Upon which he plunged himself
And sank into eternity's grand oblivion

Blood spilling with the fervor of love
Soaked the soil that held that tree

Whose xylem so engorged it raw
To paint white leaves bright red with blood

As moon broke through the parting clouds
And splashed its silvered light on down
That mulberry shone like a tomb
Above Pyramus' statured corpse

Which Thisbe saw
Across the plain
And in her grief released a wail
That took her to her bloodied knees

Showering her ravaged tresses
O'er her lover's precious face
She felt a wave of warm respite—
Until above,

The blood engorged its widest branch
Breaking loose with its own weight

To crush her skull

Ascending then together
Under waxing orb
That had shielded them
Just as anxiously with love

Crushed by the silence of gods

THE DEATH OF ORPHEUS

Beauty taunts the ignorant

And so, crooned poems of Orpheus,
More musical than common lives
Moved many against him

In great artistry
Truth will flourish
Yet spurn revenge

So, lithe and vigorous,
Orpheus spun his tales
To the pleasure of angels
And men alike

And in them he laid a road
Peppered with glory,
Of chiseled youth and firm warriors

His words, his songs,
His liquid, silken voice
Slingshot golden verse
Across admiring heavens

Slick with undulating, rippled flesh
He stood like some monolith of ancient yore

His sinewy torso wreaking majesty
Aimed at gentle men—
To the outrage of women observing:

Shunned by him for ginger boys,
They cursed his rank indifference—
For being passed by
Evokes the vengeance of woman

But he played on
And while doing so,
Maidens forged lust into weapons
That took the form of sticks and stones
Hoisted high
Where he stood on mountaintop

At first he dodged their savage moves
Till, stone by stone they had their way
Drawing blood until he fell

And when the loveliest of them all
Towered over him
And spit into his eye
Her unctuous venom

He realized his final sight
Would be her sword bringing itself
Down across his neck
Toward some separate dimension—

Gazing upside down at fish,
His head, and with it, right nearby
His holy lyre
Tossed below,
Bobbing in the sudsy foam

The river that had risen at his songs before
To overflow with surging tears
Did buoy the silenced one
Into cosseting estuaries
That gently touched the lip of waiting seas

PYGMALION OF CYPRUS

Wretched were the steps of that alter
Borne in praise of Jupiter
Where blood dripped thick and slowly
O'er its pale marble lips

Drawn not from animal veins,
It ran of human souls
Who innocently had slept within
The walls of this feigned lodging house:
The Halls of Cerastae

The monstrous ones who sewed these deeds—
Heartless, toxic vagabonds,
Minotaurs of savagery
And dirty whores—Propoetides

Venus, mocked and horrified,
Distorted them to greater depths
Of disengaged depravity:
The men were metamorphosed
Into hideous bullocks
And the women
Were recast as flint—
Malicious brittle needles

In a stunning, airy space
Above the sea
Where open, lofty rafters coaxed
The sun's bright rays to paint its walls

Worked a noble, quiet man
Whose art was made of chiseling
Our lives in stone
Where, through his magic conjuring,
As the artist at his height
Falls scarcely short of giving birth
To some new soul who seeks to speak
Yet cannot, as, without soft flesh
It cannot breathe or think or feel;
Only to repose forever
As we gaze upon its likeness
Where, perhaps through perfect stillness
We may see ourselves,
Swaddled by eternity!

—A truth we know is truthful not
Yet calms us as it signifies
We have a place among the stars
Who also die and fall to earth
While we are placed beneath its dirt
—Always well beneath these sparks

Having seen these ravages;
Repulsed by the Propoetides,
Pygmalion—musician, strings plucked by the chisel
Chose to live celibate
Rather than participate
In mediocre, fetid lust

Yet, over time
He felt within his own strong hands
Gentleness within himself
That mimicked well
The feeling of his mother's touch;
Perfumèd flowers wafting
Through pulsing, supple branches near
Intoxicating him as he did craft
The figure of a woman
From a lifeless slab

Its form, its grace was lovely to a point absurd
He could not help but fall in love
For he as man was destined to redress the womb
From light to darkness

As with all art
It saw its master passively,
Endless echoes chiding him
On waves of trepidation

One night, alone with her
While shooting stars grazed the heavens
And sprayed them both with gentle light
He raised his hand and, trembling,
Moved it to her marble breast—
Her nipple seemed to long for him;
His forefinger, the same one that had cast her forth
Touched her there
As if it had not done so
As it shaped her months ago

It circled fully hardened stone
As orbs are worshipped by their moons,
Drawing in a radiant bond
Invisible, cohesive arcs
That played a kind of music 'twixt
As silent as the galaxies

Next, he drew his lips to hers
But, just short of two mouths entwined
He paused and listened for a breath
That might prove that his masterpiece
Was 'live and ready to accept
His love, which no man ever had
In greater force for anyone

Alas—her lips remained of stone
And so, his other hand, which then
Had moved discreetly down her side
Caressing her voluptuous hip

Shaking as it lowered more,
He swiftly froze and at that point
He stood as still as whom he'd cast—
The two of them like nearby works
In some museum whose closed doors
Signified the evening hours
When they would stand in silent grace
As they had done throughout the day
When visited by those blessed
With the gift of awakening

He may have stood there until dawn;
He did not know, he did not care
He only knew that it was not
The time where he could let his love
Sing like a song of sirens

Awakened in the morning hours,
Splayed across hardened floors
The loving sun was bathing him
With rays of heated, glistening beams

He gazed on high to see her there
As light as life, yet still remiss
Of any movement other than
Her shadow, inching mystically
Across the floor below her feet
As time provoked the solar sphere

He wandered to the marketplace
And, free of thought—obsessed with love
He gathered certain lovely things:

Curios and burnished shells,
Polished stones
Snowy terns
In charming little metal jails

From the pathways he clipped flowers;
A smiling, toothless woman
In some shady stall
Sold him a pendant of Athena
And a tiny wooden, topless box
With amber paste within its walls

A jeweler showed a silver ring
That blazed in coruscation
Vibrating, sun borne rays
Danced across its deeply engraved ocean waves

With that and pearl earrings
He made his way back up the narrow lane of stone
To his bright studio

With no one near but he and she
He dressed her most adoringly,
First, with a shawl that covered her
From calf to shoulder and between

He slid two slippers on her feet
That, from Egyptian hands were weaved
And then, so gently, flowers blushed,
He slipped upon her fingers fine
That ring that dazzled passersby
Before he'd bought it for his love

Her earrings he laid gently forth,
Pretending that they hung straight down
For he could not now pierce her lobes,
Reminding him that she was naught

The rest he placed about her, near
Till all his purchases adorned
His princess as she lay there still

But after standing over her
For hours that turned the day to night
He realized that her perfection
Lay in purity, free of adornment

Seeing this, he stripped her bare
And with each move he turned his head
To leave her dignity intact—
Until the moment where, bereft
Of any fleeting vanities
She lay again, exposed to him
Upon which, almost moved to tears,

He knelt beside her, dotingly
And whispered gushing words
Of bliss below a tress that met her ear

He fell into the deepest sleep
Where time resolved
To cease its hold

Until the time that, restless still and risen up
His mind re-seized its consciousness
He ran back to the marketplace—

Day of Venus:
Throngs moved to the festival
Faithfully he led his heifer down the way
Until it stood before the goddess' shapely alter

With one swift stroke
He let its blood
And, satisfied, inflamed its corpse
As incense all about engulfed
This vicious celebration
In billows of perfumèd smoke

With pristine reverence
He arched his back and looked up high
At Venus' potent effigy
He pleaded her to gift him
With a wife—but not just any one;

He wanted her to bless with life
The one that he had sculpted there,
But feared that specificity
Might drive her to ignore his wish
And saddle him quite randomly
With some strange maiden
Who might bring
The terrors of the Propoetides
Right to his door

And so he asked that it might be
A woman who resembled well
The figure he had fashioned thus

Within a moment
Venus rose straight up
As high as Cyprus' highest tower
Flames exhausting from her mouth
And clouds of gunsmoke forming large
He felt himself upon a wind
Too strong to let him stand there firm;
Instead he turned and ran away
Back up again towards his flat

Bursting in, at sight of her,
He ran and kissed her lips with his
While, uncontrolled and in a fit
Of fear and high anxiety

He slid his hand upon her breast,
This time to feel a heat within,
Supported by a heaving breath
While from her lips tart nectar flowed
And, opening with love and wont
Her mouth was his and his was hers

Three months before a year had passed
Her wet, sweet womb
Revealed the doors of purest light

A girl named Paphos—
Now the song that is that place

MIDAS

Having showered his kindness
Upon lost Silenus
Who rambled through the hamlets
In liquored stupor
And restored him of his force,
Bacchus bestowed upon Midas
The gift of anything:
He would have his choice
Like a gourmand at grand buffets

Basking in the glory of the act
By which his minions
Had so graciously retrieved the wanderer,
The king declared his wish:
To paint with pleasure's brush
All the world in golden hues—

Avarice assumed its post
And moved the Phrygian lord
To utter his request
That he be granted instrument
To gild the world
Where'er he chose to set his hand

And so he did:
At first he touched things natural—
A peach, a plum; the ripened fig

Then he brushed a birch nearby
And turned its bark ashimmer

Kneeling down, he clawed the earth
To free up fragile peonies—
Underneath his royal nails
The powdery soil turned sparkly dust

And as he stepped toward his home
His feet embossed their molded prints
With golden leaf
That flashed the brilliant light of sun
Into the eyes of Bacchus,
Now concerned this foolish king
Would leave his mark across the land
Without discretion—
Only with the seed that men
Would follow near
To peel away and take for theirs

To wit: He touched the castle door
And bronzed knob recast itself
Into a glimmering, massive piece
Of gold, the size of which he leered
Before entering to the hall
From which he ran through chambers dark
To meditate on what to do;
On how to stop this foolish scene

That now quite soon
Could end with he himself recast
Into some tragic statue
Of his living self
That men might tear asunder
And with greed, reduce to handy nuggets
Perfect for the marketplace

He knew now that his fate was sealed;
For when he plied himself with wine
To soothe his heart and misery
It dried into a splendid arc
That choked his throat and stole his wind

He threw himself upon his bed
Which just as quickly turned
To precious, glistened metal beneath him

At the tail of night
Just before a lip of sun
Had tweaked the sky with yellow breath,
The tortured king
Escaped with shame
His very own high habitat
And as he scaled down the wall
At quarters rear, remote from sight
The stone itself was turned to gold;
No sooner had he reached the woods
Than morning light

Had set this vacant citadel
Ablaze in golden luster

Into shadowed thickets he absconded
And lay upon the ground to weep
Until his tears—themselves of gold
Ran downward to the valley floor
And formed a babbling brook
That trickled o'er the plain
Until it passed the feet
Of noble Bacchus
Who had followed it back up the rise
And through a dale
Where, on the sod,
Amongst the flowers,
He found the king in full despair—

Midas, now a hollow man
Threw himself at Bacchus' feet
Begging that he cure him of
The cursed gift of riches

Pitying the fallen head,
The heartful God of Ecstasy
Pointed Midas up the hills
To Sardis
Where a river ran from shining peaks
There, he said, go plunge yourself
Beneath the waters from its falls—

It shall bathe away your cursed gift
And cast you to its riverbed
A man free of such alchemy

Midas, with this pilgrimage
Stayed up within the shadowed woods
Ascetic now and fearful of
The very sight of golden hues
Even shimmering tones within the setting sun
Enough to send a shudder
Through his aged spine

But Midas was, to Jove, an ass—
He could not help but probe once more
And this time into leagues
Far above his human station

He strolled about one summer's day
Across a ridge that looked down sharply
On the hamlet of Hypaepa
Whose people went about their business
While, high above,
Pan began to play a song of love
From his lovely sterling pipe

Tmolus, mountain god of Lydia
Watched with the Hypaepeans
As the glorious piper declared
That even Apollo found it well

To make use of his melodies,
Sweeter than any nectar they were

It stunned him to look forth and see
The stark stone face of Apollo

Set against cerulean sky—
Grim and cross,
Having heard the galimatias
Of shabby Midas,
Once the gilded king
Ghastly now, clad in rags
Imbedded with fine grains of gold—
The last marks of wealth

In godly rage,
Son of elegant Leto
Held his torch
High above the head of Midas
Releasing roars that thundered so,
They shook the shale from pitched fjords
And tore the skin off oranges and nectarines
On trees that lined the shores below

With this a cloud of smoke arose
Surrounding the dim, hapless king
And when it cleared with upper gusts
That raked the hills with chilly air
The first thing that those gods about

Did see with their amazed eyes,
Keen as the eyes of Naso,
Were donkey's ears, full of fur
That sat atop the frightened head
Of poor, pathetic Midas

He slowly rolled his eyes up high
And saw within his widest view
Their tips—his tips—
Branding him an ass forever,
Having never listened
And having never heard
The lovely music of Apollo

ACTAEON

Nature is an abattoir
We are its butchers

Actaeon, like cattle for slaughter
Knew not that one random day
Would bring him to the doors of death

So he strode within the shadowed envelope
Of forest pines;
Late on one moist autumn day
Down the hill behind his troupe
Rolled great smooth balls of greyish mist—
Above, a cloudy blanket wringed its waters down
In tickling, chilly droplets

Surrounded by his faithful hounds
And breathing in the thickish, heady balsam air
He stepped with joy upon
Caramel needles of bristly pine

Through the morn and then the day
His arrows soared both to and fro
As stripling deer and bullish boar
Fell on stumbling, numbed knees
Led by time into the darkest world

They stopped to rest in growing heat
Upon the foothills of Gargaphie
Where Actaeon,
Reaching into bloody sack
Declared to his companions
That they should retreat—
Their loads full of fresh ripe game,
Enough to feed their tribe
For a full fortnight

They dropped their kill
Around which
Their drooling dogs surrounded,
Dropping to their sweated loins
To form a circle
Within which carcasses
Pierced by masterly arrows
Mourned themselves

Far within the cavern grand
They'd entered from its western mouth
Lay golden grotto
Where bright-flecked canaries
Sang in tones so lush
Ivy leaves upon the rocky walls did blush

Within that pristine, sacred vault—
Below its upper craggy lip
Chiseled with such love and awe,

Beside the foot of smoothened pond
Whose surface was so slick and still
Stood the most glorious of maidens
Like a statue that could breathe:
Lips sacchariferous,
Shoulders graceful and sublime
Nectarous Aphrodite
Lush spectre,
Rhapsodic nymph

Attended by six abigails
Who washed her feet with earthen pails
Her privacy complete,
She felt a rush of ecstasy

The supple breeze about her
Carried wisps of vetiver and milk flower

Through a peaceful glade of birch
Tucked within her sacred combe
Spread a ray of warming light
Pure as the star from which it burst
Leading like a lure
The eye of Actaeon

Hypnotic beam, cursed tempter
With no mind as such
Shall you ever know
The blood that you would cause to spill—

As this flowing, molten lux,
Like a river to the sea
Is buoyed by one current
Yet lays a path the other way
For he who seeks to fight the spate,
Provided course of vision
Upon which the golden eyes of Aphrodite
Did meet head on those of the huntsman

And at that crucial moment
His heart was seized by mirth, while groomed for death

The fall of honor is one so great
It tears the bottom of one's heart
To seep cruor upon the frozen fields
Thus was the loss of Aphrodite:
Her virtue was the badge of every worthy maiden—
The muliebrity of mothers

With such flagrant violation,
Soul a shambles,
The fine goddess rose up—
Fathoms tall
In the eyes of her virgin nymphs

Her voice, no normal, chipper tone—
Booming admonitions,
It pierced the rocky halls like thunder

Calling to great Jupiter
To seize the form of Actaeon
And cast him forth as wild stag—

Quite suddenly he stood on fours,
Antlers twisting to and fro
Taking in the frantic scene
While, before his startled eyes
His hounds had turned to face him, near—
Their jowls awash, hankering;
Their drooling fangs
Prepared to turn upon their master—now a beast

He bolted for the cavern mouth
But was no match
For the heat of dogs
Who took him down upon the earth which had spawned him

NIOBE

King Amphion's wife was Niobe
She bore him fourteen children

Her pride of family pedigree
Far trumped that for her offspring

Manto, insane innocent
Daughter to Tiresias

Whose vision was the future, now,
Cast upon the Theban women
Shrieks she claimed to be the voice
Of Leto, glorious goddess
Who through Jupiter
Spawned their lovely, fearsome twins
Apollo and Artemis

Her startling, heartfelt pleas
Commanded them to seek the shrine
And leave behind burnt offerings
To that deified family

And so they did:

The youngest ones
Set bouquets of lavender

And cardamom to flame
While elders stooped above the stones
To chant in whispered rhapsodies
Praise and reverence
For Leto of the Titans

As they moved so gracefully
Without a sound
Beneath the vaulted shelter
Of their temple
Which graced the hills
Above the rhythmic, lapping sea,

Niobe, wrapped in gilded gold—
Shimmering fatality,
Ascended barren temple steps
Entering the sacred hall
Where devotees
Ensconced in ministrations
To their cherished goddess
Did not at first
Look up to see her towering above:
The sheer force of her arrogance
Had coaxed her slender frame
To grow on upwards
Like a tree that,
Right before their eyes
Transformed itself in minutes few
To span above the highest mount

And gaze upon the vales below
With scorn and disenchantment great

She spoke to them in wicked tone:
You pray to empty, hollow shrines;
To someone who is not above—
What fools you are to think that she
Is in the misty, banded belt
Of ether that protects this sphere
On which you dwell so feebly
While, before you
I here stand
To demonstrate that fate as well
Is folly great and nothing more:
For, I, a queen of noble blood
With honored house and many jewels
Created with my body pure
The greatest treasure known to man:
A family of many heads—
Seven girls and seven boys,
Each one brighter than the last—
Panoply of glistening stars

Stay here though and burn your bows;
Pray to ears as deaf as wood
While I regale with power and pride
About the shining horn of plenty
Knowing that, like our legacy
My precious, dazzling offspring

Is worthy of Zeus' praise—
As is my House of Amphion

Cowering under brazen words
The suppliants cast flowered offerings
About the alter floor
Before abandoning their temple

And although they removed themselves
To show an empty vestibule,
Within their hearts
Their fever for sweet Leto
Kept its scorching pitch;
Their prayers mellifluous upon
A hidden belt of energy
That laced itself above the tower
Ascending to the darkest sky
As evening set upon the streets of Thebes
And people there

Atop snowy Cynthus
Leto stood and heard their pleas
Fury from her lips did leave
And take the shape of bronzed trumpets
Heralding her striking twins, Apollo and Artemis

Soaring through the heavens high
They beckoned to her rousing calls:
If you love me as you say,
If my heart and womb are yours;
If you know our deity
And if you cherish all we are
Know that Niobe, that wench,
Boastfully has claimed to all
Her kingdom
As the hall
Highest in the vaulted skies—
Greater than my palace too?!

Seek her out and let her learn
Truth in its most brazen form:
Take from her what she holds dear—
Robbed then of her earthly things
She will learn respect and awe
Leave no stone unturned in this—
For your mother's sake and yours
Let the ground beneath them
Rock the House of Tantalus
And have it roll to rubble
At the base of pounding seas

With this her children mounted steeds
Of blazing white fair coats, pristine

Gliding high above the hills
They soon were hovering above
Temperate Thebes—

Across its splendid, fertile plains,
Betwixt the farms and garden belts
There were equestrian fields and runs
Upon which, blissfully from on high
Mares and steeds all pranced about
Sat upon by strong, sweet youth—
Children of great Amphion
And Niobe, boastful bride

Galloping about the land,
Gently fading sunbeams warm
Upon their shining faces pure,
Each was quite content and set
Reveling in nature's play

When the first great arrow struck Ismenus,
Eldest son of all
Blood splashed so fiercely across the clouds
That towns were cast in crimson tint
As lovely light was tarnished red—
It pierced earth's foggy banks

Next it was young Sipylus:
As he galloped joyfully
Across the meadows parting hills

Near Maeonia,

What first appeared to be a hawk
Screamed high across the sky above—
All looked up from the stables,
Covering their ears and cowering
At a sound louder than ever heard

It was a lofty boomerang
That curved and arced with godly grace
On path so clear
Its victim saw death before himself
Well before it came down
And swept his head from twisting shoulders
Sending it straight out from earth
—It took to the moon
And forevermore could be seen
As that gibbous face
When peaked tides broach the shores of Athens

So was the fate for the next four sons of crass Niobe:
Each knocked down upon the earth
From prancing steeds,
Veins opened; limbs flailing
—Hearts brought to eternity

The winds of death
Blew so rich across these fallow plains

That ranks of elm trees
All at once
Bowed their bows towards the open lands
In mourning for their fallen ones

A final quiver left Apollo's hand
Blazing through the air so steadfastly
Smoke was seen emitting from its tail
Turning back to look, with fear
Riding with keen fury
In flight from this mass butchery,
Damasichthon twisted his stately head
Around to see the golden arrow
Coming to its fateful end
Sky blue left eye
Exploding into silence

The Niobids half vanquished,
Artemis set her sights upon the daughters,
Seven strong—
Screaming from the stables
They scattered in the woodlands
Tender feet pierced by needles
—Scurrying across the pungent forest floor

Slayer of Actaeon,
Princess of beauty
Caster of light—
Sororal septet, struck down

With all the vengeance of woman
Aphrodite obeyed her mother's command

Now every girl sprung from the womb of Niobe
Lay with buttery cheek to the firmament

Niobe, fit to picnic
With her spawn,
Graced in lovely, bejeweled robes
Discovered blood-soaked fields
—A beck of blood
Leading to a mellow glen
Upon which lay in piles
Her savaged spawn

Wailing with a howl
That pierced the heavens
She threw herself in morbid grief
Against a wall of soaring stone
In fusion with the edifice

Niobe's grief was for all time—
Her tears turned to rain
That soaked the hinterlands
And flooded crops

Queen of Thebes,
Matron of Lydia,
Bound by motionless sorrows

When her tears had dried up,
All her self hardened
With the bond of rigorous metals

Passersby from then till now
May see at times
Her tears streaming anew

Misery timeless

CYGNUS

Warrior, son of Neptune
Sweeping his sword about the air,
Left in his trail
A thousand heads of Grecians—
Sparkling sabre, wet with blood

Rivers red,
Coagulate with crimson paste:
Louros, like the cardinal's wing
Krios and Krathis—
Mornos overflowing,
Flooded by their flowing veins
Erubescent rivulets

Cygnus, quite impervious
Stood on hilltop t'wards the next
Facing great Achilles
Who challenged him and raised his spear

Laughing, Cygnus shrugged him off
Boasting of his father's realm:
To you, my skin is steel
Your blades will split,
Your arrows fail:
My heart is locked within
This bronzed chest
No man nor god can penetrate

With this the forceful Achilles
Stood tall and spoke his part:

As I slew Hector
I shall now show
To all the world
The vigor that I bring to bear
Upon those that would rape this land
And dare to mow our soldiers down
As if they were but daffodils
Upon these sacred plains of Jove

With one splendid motion
Olympian in grace and bite
He thrust his golden spear
Across the valley with such force,
A short-toed eagle
Flew up off his lofty perch
So as to flee the rod

To his perturbation
It bounced off the armored chest of Cygnus
Who roared with glee:
I cannot be touched;
Only but I can touch, he boasted

Looking down upon the hills
He noticed movement in the heather—

There strode Menoetes,
Shepherd with harsh oxen,
Blackened coats and evil eyes—
Leading Pluto's cattle
To the gates of hell

Again Achilles raised his arm
And let loose his spear
That, flying faster than sound
Struck with mighty thunderclap,
Ripping out the heart of Menoetes,
Pinning it to a sycamore

Confidence and will restored,
Great son of Thetis, warrior king
Grasped again his loyal spear
—With still more might than his last cast
He aimed with deadly, driven eye
And hurled it forth with such great whirl
That thunderbolts returned above
While clouds grew gray with edgy haze

Once again
His spear was impotent—
What, he pondered;
Is perhaps my human side—
I, son of mortal Peleus,
Abandoning my sacred needs
As I have never seen before?

At loss to find a remedy
And, given all his building rage
He lunged upon the smug, rude foe
Madness seizing his huge heart—
He pounced and pounded foe
So long and so hard
That seasons changed;
The summer winds gave way to squalls and stormy heights
And then, piece by piece
The armor and garb of Cygnus
Did loosen and begin to shatter;
Blood ran forth from every limb—
The vanquished victim underneath
Was finally still;
No more laughter teased the skies

Finally paused, retrieving breath
Achilles smacked the helmet off—
He looked aghast to see
Nothingness within its bowl

A giant egret—
Flapping colossus
Sleek as the longest galley
Cutting course above the waves,
High above a trail within the soaring depths below—

A silken flounder
Stomach tickled by the sands
That gave the sea its bottom

Corals, washed in pinkish veil
Of pale blood
Fresh from the gills
Of this bruised fish

Headed to his watery cathedral

Terrified a second time,
The eagle at high noon
Gazed out to see from jagged cliff
This godly scene

Sirocco buffeting itself
Towards the ravaged lands

❧ EPILOGUES ❧

Creation

Peleus and Thetis

Proserpina

Thisbe

Death of Orpheus

Pygmalion

Midas

Tears of Actaeon

Niobe

Cygnus

CREATION

Resonance—
Stark canyons, maroon bells

Acrid void
Lilies, mountains, oceans, air
From nothing to nothing
Cape of consciousness
Great colossus
      Let your rivers flow
      From your sacred brine,
Light, lux, lumen:
Lead us to your emerald vaults—
Sisi on the mast

Jupiter:
What will you do when I die?

PELEUS AND THETIS

Vile spawn
Engorged upon Thetis' flesh
—The flesh of every woman

Mothers, sisters, daughters
None are free

Emerald canyons,
Granite suite held no steed
Against a course of lust and will

PROSERPINA

Torched isle
Mouth of lava
Scorched heavens

Skin of Sicily
Dry and shattered—
Turned to dust

Typhon rising
Rains upon the warming seas

Catanians, Siracusans
Washed away; Pluto vanquished

Swans of Pergusa
—They knew only spring

THISBE

Minute fissure
Gentle daggers, splintered light

Love of lovely tender years
The lynx' great paw
Blazing arbor

Floundering in bloody pond,
Pyramus pursued his love

Mountain—
She within its rigid bowels
Grasping still their flaming torch

Souls departed, self-extinguished
In the time of love and honor

DEATH OF ORPHEUS

Holy, sweet hymn
Tossed out on the open air
Beauty swayed,
Holy lyre
Sonorous—abandoned hearts
Swaths of oaks
Sweetly swollen, swooning riffs

Beasts descending,
Beauty swayed
Nature's darkest perfumed plague
Tore the flesh of Orpheus

Eyes locked, fixed on stars—
Pleiades fading

Music sings of death and rapture
Songs sung through the lilies,
Egrets;
Lilac lips

Lay your song upon my breast

PYGMALION

Sanguine steps, crimson pools
Sons and daughters
Throats turned out to satiate
Foul conundrum,
Sea of whores
Madness surging;
Hopeful heart

Metamorphosis:
Requite-resolute-recalcitrant
Venusian pyre—
Within the goddess' gaze,
Reverie of honeyed mirth
Consumed soul
—Embers feel the chilly bath
Of fleeting bliss

MIDAS

Gold: shield of avarice
Richly hue
Infected, foolish Midas—
Lava coursing through his veins

Metaled blood—shimmering glow

No person, place or thing
Held its place unlacquered

TEARS OF ACTAEON

Smothered by wonder, he stopped—

Ascending stately thigh; insatiable
Heated loins caressed;
A wash of warmth
Uncoiling from her silken flesh
To prance across the forest floor
And tear his throat
Within her womb,
A mile from fear—

The justice of hounds

NIOBE

Sweet Letos
Temple pastoral
Vows and prayers;
Golden bulb

Father descended,
Brackish pool,
Fruits denied

O'er the hill,
Mountainous rise,

Leto's babes,
Talons dipped in molten gold
Razor tips—
Fourteen hearts

The dead matter

CYGNUS

Shadowed heel,
Hammered blows
Blue sphere of Neptune

Crimson streams
Lovelier than sunbeams
—Blood of the privileged son

Great Godhead,
            Mad Achilles
Depths and shallows unknown

Peter Shaindlin divides his time between fine art photography, writing and working to foster awareness of the arts and their cultural underpinnings in both the community and education. He is a visiting fellow at Harris Manchester College, University of Oxford. Originally from New York, he resides in Honolulu, Hawaii.

BIBLIOGRAPHY

Metamorphoses (Latin text), Ovid (Publius Ovidius Naso), thelatinlibrary.com.

Metamorphoses, Ovid (Publius Ovidius Naso),
Penguin Books, 2004, Translated by David Raeburn.

Tales from Ovid, Ted Hughes, 1997, Farrar, Straus
and Giroux.

www.ingramcontent.com/pod-product-compliance
Lightning Source LLC
La Vergne TN
LVHW091217080426
835509LV00009B/1040